The Environment

KU-017-699

Contents

Revision

Did you know . . . ?

⭐ **There are different kinds of environment.**

⭐ **Living things are adapted to their environment.**

⭐ **Plants and animals in a habitat depend upon each other.**

 Task 1

Different environments

 Look at the photos on pages 2 and 3.

 Write down the different environments you can see.

 A habitat is part of the environment. Write about some of the different habitats that you might find in these environments.

 What sort of living things do you think there are in the different habitats?

 How do you think they are adapted to their environment?

 PCM 1

 Use the table on Photocopy Master 1 to show how the plants and animals have adapted.

Animal/ plant name	How has it adapted to where it lives?
Snail	Shell – to protect it from drying out. Colour – to provide camouflage.

Task 2

Food chains and food webs

 Is the fox a carnivore or herbivore? Is it a predator? Name some prey of the fox. Make a food chain for the fox.

 Now make a food web for the fox.

⭐ Habitats change.

Salt-marsh habitat

Look at the photograph. It shows a grass which lives in a salt marsh. The grass has adapted to living in a soil that has a lot of salt in it. Most plants around your home and school will not be able to live in salty soil. It would make them wilt, dry up and die.

Habitats can change however. This investigation shows you what would happen to a potato plant if its natural habitat changed and became more salty.

you need:

- a team of Star Investigators
- a potato
- a potato peeler
- a knife and cutting board
- a tablespoon
- some plastic containers
- water
- salt

PLANNING BOARD

Our question _____
We will change _____
We will measure _____

We will keep _____
these things _____
the same to _____
make our test _____
fair _____

This is the
table we
will use.
(Put in the
headings.
Fill in the
left-hand
column.)

We will use _____
these things _____

Task 3   **Investigation**
Different conditions for potato chips

① In your group, take a potato and use a potato peeler to peel it.

② Ask your teacher to cut it into chips.

③ Take two bowls or plastic containers and label them 'water' and 'salt water'.

④ Put about 5 cm of water in each (just enough to cover the chips when you add them).

⑤ Add three heaped tablespoons of salt to make the salt water. Stir in the salt to dissolve it.

⑥ Make two piles of six chips of about the same size.

Weigh each pile and record the weight in a table like the one on page 5.
Use Photocopy Master 2.

⑦ Add six chips to the water and six to the salt water.

⑧ Note what time it is and leave them for 30 minutes.

⑨ Take the chips out of the water and soak up the drips on some kitchen paper.

Weigh them, record the weight and return them to their container.

Repeat for the chips in the salt water.

Safety point: Be very careful with the knife and peeler.

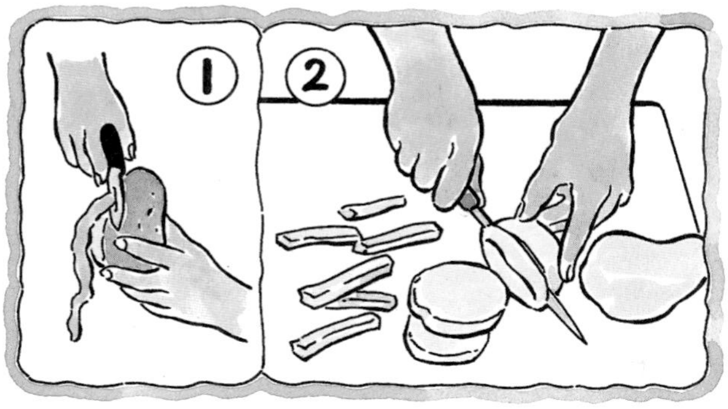

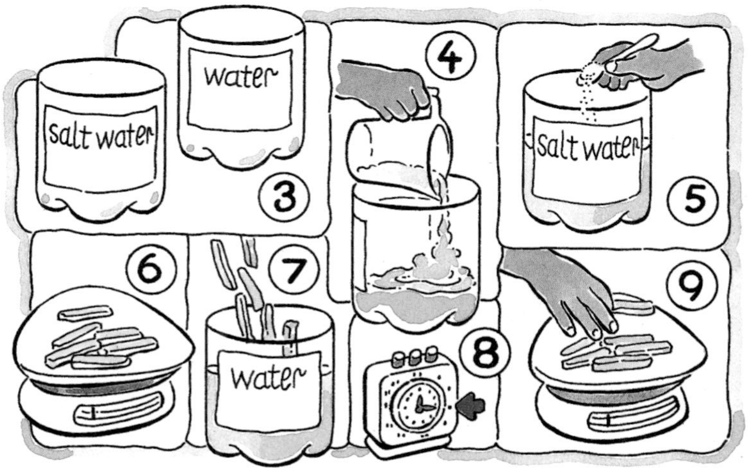

- Weigh both piles of chips again after another 30 minutes (one hour from the start).
- Fill in the rest of the table.
- Use the information to help you work out how the weight of the chips changes.

Answer these questions.

① What did the chips in the water feel like after 30 minutes?

② What did they feel like after one hour?

③ What did the chips in the salt water feel like after one hour?

④ What was the only difference in the way the chips were treated?

⑤ Why do you think some chips gained weight?

⑥ Why do you think some chips lost weight?

Weight of chips in water:	**Weight of chips in salt water:**
At start: ________ g	At start: ________ g
Weight after 30 mins: ________ g	Weight after 30 mins: ________ g
Change in weight: ________ g	Change in weight: ________ g
Weight after 60 mins: ________ g	Weight after 60 mins: ________ g
Total change in weight: ________ g	Total change in weight: ________ g

Now try this

Task 4

Looking at other groups' results

✦ What did the other groups in the class find out from their investigation in Task 3?

✦ Design a table to show their readings so that you have a set of repeat readings for changes in the weight of the chips.

✦ Find the average change in weight, after one hour, for the chips in water and the chips in salt water for all groups in the class.

✦ Put your results on a bar chart showing how the weight of the chips changed in:
• water
• salt water.

✦ Remember, some of the chips got lighter while others got heavier. Why did these changes happen? Draw or write to show what happened.

Task 5

Salty soil

✦ Read the Fact File. Why do you think the farmers cannot use the land straight away?

✦ What would happen if potatoes were planted in salty soil?

✦ Write down your ideas about how the land might become less and less salty so that farmers could use it for growing crops.

Fact File

Land reclaimed from the sea

In parts of Lincolnshire and Norfolk, crops are grown on land that was once part of the sea. Barriers have been built to keep out the sea and the land has been drained. This is called **reclaimed land**.

Reclaimed land cannot be used for growing crops straight away.

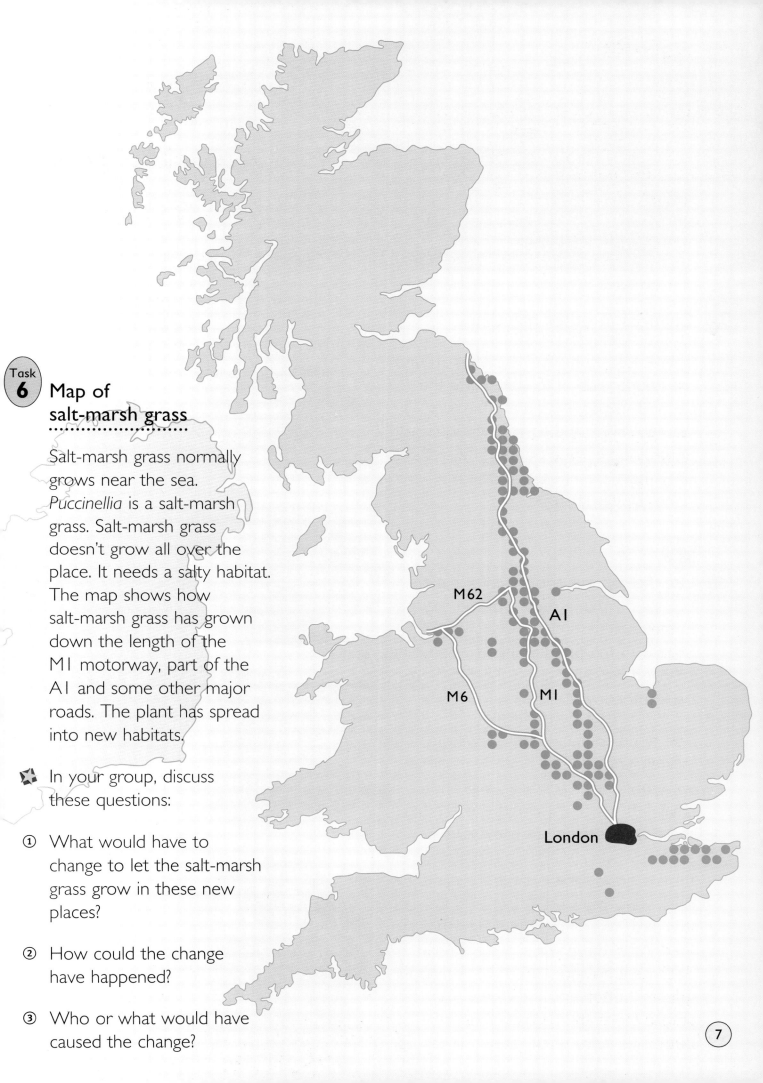

Map of salt-marsh grass

Salt-marsh grass normally grows near the sea. *Puccinellia* is a salt-marsh grass. Salt-marsh grass doesn't grow all over the place. It needs a salty habitat. The map shows how salt-marsh grass has grown down the length of the M1 motorway, part of the A1 and some other major roads. The plant has spread into new habitats.

In your group, discuss these questions:

① What would have to change to let the salt-marsh grass grow in these new places?

② How could the change have happened?

③ Who or what would have caused the change?

M62

A1

M6

M1

London

Changes in other habitats

There used to be lots of ponds around the countryside in the UK. After the Second World War, many farmers wanted more land to grow food crops. Some filled in their ponds. The pictures show how the habitats of the filled in ponds slowly changed.

 Use the pictures and the information below to make a record of the changes in the habitats.
Start with the pond and end when it has changed into a meadow. Use the table on Photocopy Master 3.

The pond contained lots of wildlife including pondweed, waterlilies, larvae, waterboatmen, tadpoles, frogs and small fish. Once the pond was filled in, there was nothing but bare soil for several weeks. After two months, thistles, couch-grass, dandelions and dock were growing. A few wild animals and birds visited the changing habitat to feed. After three years, the area had become a meadow filled with meadow grasses, buttercups and clover. Cows grazed there and rabbits, birds and butterflies were often seen.

You can set up your own observations to see how parts of a garden habitat change.

✿ With permission, choose an area of garden, at school or at home, half a metre square (50 cm x 50 cm).

✿ Take out all the plants so that the soil is bare.

✿ You could divide this habitat into squares, using string.

✿ Label each square, for example, A, B, C, and so on.

✿ Use a table to record where plants begin to grow. Use Photocopy Master 4.

Square	Number of plants after 1 week	Number of plants after 2 weeks	Number of plants after 4 weeks
A	1		
B	0		
C	0		
D	2		
E	0		
F	1		

✿ Try to identify the plants as they grow. Record your findings like this:

Type of plant	After 1 week	After 2 weeks	After 4 weeks
Dandelion	1	3	7
Groundsel	2	4	5
Can't identify			

Fact File

Lichens

Lichens are a mixture of two kinds of living things: **algae**, which are tiny coloured plants that normally live in water and **fungi** which live on rotting things.

Together, they can live in places such as on rocks and walls where it is difficult for other plants to grow.

Lichens were the first plants to begin growing after the last **Ice Age**. In Lapland, where it is very cold, reindeer feed on lichens. ▶

A new gravestone or stone wall has very little living on it. But, slowly, lichens can start to grow on some gravestones or walls.

There are three types of lichen:

- **Flat** lichens
- **Leafy** lichens
- **Shrubby** lichens.

Flat lichens look like 'crazy paving' when viewed with a magnifying glass.

Leafy lichens are flat, leafy plants with fat rounded parts that look like leaves. They can be orange-yellow, grey, brown or black.

Shrubby lichens are also known as beard lichens. They are very small bushy plants with branches.

Investigation

Habitats for lichens

A gravestone is a good habitat for lichens. You can use this habitat for many investigations. Try this one.

> Find out whether how old a gravestone is, makes a difference to the number of lichens growing on it.

you need:
- a team of Star Investigators
- clip board and paper
- pens and pencils

- Study four gravestones for your investigation.

- Use a planning board to help you.

- How will you work out the age of the gravestones?

- How will you make your investigation fair?

- Will you look at the whole of the gravestone or just a small area?

- Collect your information.

PCM 5

- Record the information in a table using Photocopy Master 5.

Oldest date on gravestone	Age of gravestone	Number of lichens
1.		
2.		

- Draw a graph of your results. What sort of graph will you draw? Why?

- Look for a pattern on your graph. Tell the story of your graph.

This is what some year 5 children think about **microbes**.

> Microbes are just bits of dust you see in sunbeams.

> Microbes are dead.

> Microbes are horrible germs which make us poorly!

> My grandfather says some germs are good for us.

Read the Fact File and see if you agree with them.

Micro-organisms

Micro-organisms are everywhere.
They are often called microbes or germs.
They are the smallest of all living things.
You need a microscope to see most of them.

There are four types of microbe. They have been magnified hundreds of times to take these photos:

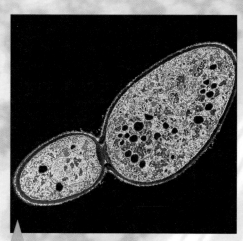

fungi

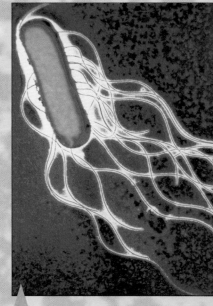

bacteria

viruses

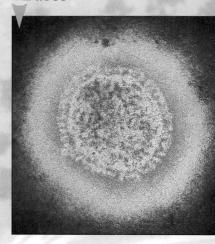

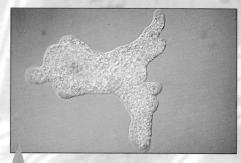

protozoa (animals made of one cell, for example, amoeba)

Useful microbes

Some microbes are useful.

Yeast is a microbe. It is a **fungus**. It is used every day to make bread, beer and wine. In Brazil, they use yeast to make alcohol and mix it with petrol to make a fuel called 'gasohol'. It is cleaner than using ordinary petrol.

Bacteria and fungi rot things and cause them to decay. This can be useful. For example, decaying things are used for making compost for gardens. Bacteria also causes sewage to rot.

On some farms, bacteria are mixed with animal waste to make natural gas.
The farmers use it as a source of energy.
Some **viruses** are used by plant breeders to make unusual flowers, for example, different patterns and colours in flowers such as tulips. Myxomatosis is a virus that was used to kill rabbits when they were seen as pests in the 1950s.

Fungus growing on horse manure

Harmful microbes

Some microbes are harmful and cause diseases, for example, chickenpox, colds, flu, mumps and meningitis.

When we are ill, the environment in our body changes for a time. We may become hotter and have a temperature of more than 37 °C – which is normal body temperature. This is our body's way of trying to kill the microbes causing the illness.

Task
10 The uses of microbes
·······················

PCM
6

 Use the Fact File to fill in the table on Photocopy Master 6.

 Paint a large picture or make a collage to show what each microbe looks like.

Type of microbe	Uses	Describe what it looks like
	To make bread, wine and beer	
Viruses		
Bacteria		

13

◆ Now try this

You found out in the Fact File on page 13 that yeast is a microbe.

✸ Your teacher may be able to let you look at some yeast under a microscope.

✸ Use Photocopy Master 7 to help you.

✸ Put some grains of dried yeast in 20 ml of water.

✸ Stir and leave for 30 minutes.

✸ Use a pipette to put a drop of the mixture on to a microscope slide. Cover it with a cover slip.

✸ Look at it under the microscope.

✸ Draw what you see.

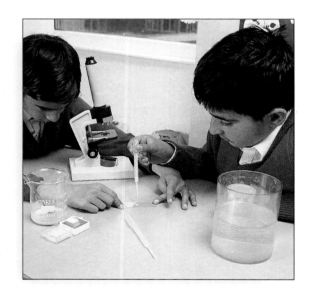

Using bacteria

you need:

- a team of Star Investigators
- some disinfectant
- a mixing bowl
- a cloth for mopping up spills

Either:

- 750 ml (1.5 pints) of sterilized milk (UHT)

or

- 750 ml of water and 125 g of powdered milk
- six plastic cups or glass cups
- clingfilm
- a balloon whisk
- a yoghurt maker or thermos flask/jug
- teaspoon
- jug
- 'live' natural yoghurt
- a pH meter or pH paper

Task 11 — Using bacteria to change a milky habitat!

Microbes change things around them. In the investigation on the following four pages you are going to find out how special yoghurt bacteria make changes to a milky habitat.

Yoghurt is made by bacteria changing some of the substances in milk.

In a warm milk and live natural yoghurt mixture, the yoghurt bacteria multiply very quickly.

The bacteria change the sugar in milk into a mild **acid**. This is what makes the yoghurty taste. ▶

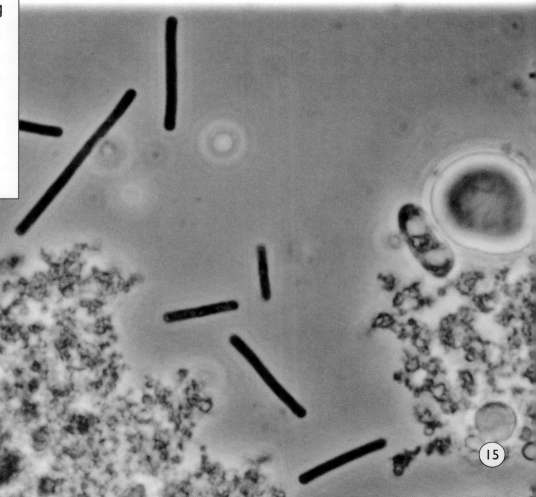

Using bacteria

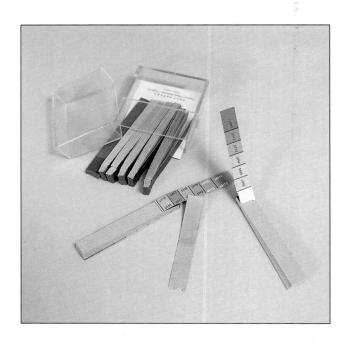

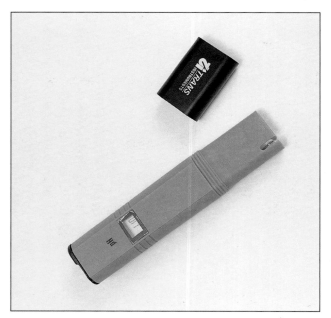

Before you begin the investigation, you need to know how to measure how acid things are.

We can measure this with either a pH meter or pH paper. When the pH paper is dipped into a liquid, the paper changes colour. The colour changes are compared with colours on a chart. The pH meter reads the pH and displays it digitally.

- A pH of **more** than 7 means the liquid is **alkaline**. Soapy things and toothpaste are alkaline. It is the opposite of acid.

- A pH of **less** than 7 means the liquid is **acid**. Vinegar and lemon juice are acid. It is the opposite of alkaline.

- A pH of **7** means the liquid is **neutral**. It is neither acid nor alkaline. Pure (or distilled) water is neutral. Tap water is slightly alkaline.

Practise finding the pH of some liquids using either a pH meter or pH paper, or both. Use Photocopy Master 8.

Record the results in a table like this:

Substance	pH reading	Acid or alkaline?
Tap water		
Washing-up liquid		

- Now, make the yoghurt.

- Wipe your work surface with the disinfectant to kill any microbes.

- Decide whether to use UHT or powdered milk.

- Put the milk into a mixing bowl.

- Put two tablespoons of the milk into a jug.

- Add two teaspoons of live natural yoghurt to the jug and stir in.

- Add this yoghurt mixture to the milk in the mixing bowl.

- Whisk with a balloon whisk.

- If you are using a yoghurt maker, add nearly all the milk mixture to the cups. Keep some to test the pH. Cover the cups with clingfilm.

- Then ask your teacher to plug in the yoghurt maker.

- If you do not have a yoghurt maker, use the warmest place in the school or place the mixture in a clean thermos flask.

- It will take about eight hours to make the yoghurt.

Using bacteria

✦ Every hour remove a sample of yoghurt from the same pot to test the pH. Wipe the pH meter probe with disinfectant each time, to kill any microbes, or use a clean piece of pH paper each time.

✦ Test the pH of the yoghurt as accurately as you can with the pH meter or paper.

✦ Record any changes in pH and the texture or appearance of the milk and live yoghurt mixture. Use Photocopy Master 9.

Write down your answers to these questions.

① How does the milk mixture change as the yoghurt is made?

② What was the pH of the milk at the start?

③ What was the pH of the milk at the end?

④ What do you think has caused the milk to change into yoghurt?

Time (hours)	pH reading	What is the mixture like?
start 0		
1		
2		
3		
4		
5		
6		
7		
8		

Fact File

Decaying plants

When a living thing dies, it **decays**.
Microbes, such as bacteria and fungi,
help to rot dead plants and animals.
Think about what the world would look
like if things didn't decay!

you need:

• some oak or sycamore leaves

• hair nets or old fruit nets

• some things that you would usually throw away e.g. empty fizzy drinks cans, old plastic carrier bags, old sweet wrappers

• a place with some damp soil.

Task 12 Decaying things

 Collect oak or sycamore leaves and put them into a hair net or fruit net.

 Find a place with damp soil and bury the net. Mark the place where you buried it.

 In another net bury some other things that we usually throw away – for example, old cans, sweet wrappers. Mark the place.

 Look at the nets each week.

 What changes do you notice?

 Record the changes that you see in a table like this:

Safety note: Wear plastic or rubber gloves when you are working with soil. Wash your hands afterwards.

Write down your answers to these questions:

① Which things decay?

② Which things appear not to decay?

③ What makes the decay happen?

④ How are microbes involved?

⑤ How could you make some things decay more quickly?

Material	Date:	Date:	Date:	Date:	Date:
Leaves					
Cans					
Plastic bags					

An environment is a system which can be harmed.

Ecosystems

Living things depend upon each other.

They also depend on things that are not alive, for example, air and water. Together, these living and non-living things form **ecosystems**.

The living things in an ecosystem include plants and animals which make food chains and food webs. The non-living things include oxygen, carbon dioxide, water and light. If the environment is harmed, the ecosystem and the life in it is also harmed.

A pond is an example of an ecosystem.

Read this story.

Disaster at Heron Pond

1 Lots of animals live in or around Heron Pond. The pond helps them to stay alive.

Heron Pond is near a tractor shed. Fuels, oils, insecticides and weed killers are kept near the shed.

2 One of the containers with oil in it was damaged. It leaked oil.

The oil trickled down the path towards the pond.

6 The children told Farmer Brown about the oil.

7 I know what we can do to help. We'll get some detergent from the house and put that on the pond.

Farmer Brown thought of a way of cleaning the pond.

In your group, talk about what Farmer Brown and the children could do.

3 The oil formed a film on the surface of the pond. This made it hard for air to get into the water.

The ducks' feathers became covered with oil.

4 Below the surface of the pond, the fish were beginning to find it difficult to breathe.

Help!

The water boatman could not collect fresh oxygen for its air bubble.

5 Some children came to stay at the farm near Heron Pond.

They noticed the oil trickling down to the pond.

8 The animals in the pond were now really in trouble.

But won't the detergent harm the animals?

9 Stop! There must be other ways you can help us!

Will this help? The animals in the pond are very worried!

PCM 10

✪ Write to show your ideas. Use Photocopy Master 10.

✪ Collect all your ideas together. Tasks 14 –17 may help you to try out some of your ideas.

(23)

you need:

- a team of Star Investigators
- one type of plant e.g. duckweed or cress
- one detergent e.g. washing powder or washing-up liquid
- 5 beakers (or cut down fizzy drinks bottles) each containing 100 ml water
- plastic or rubber gloves

Safety note: Use plastic or rubber gloves when handling detergents.

PLANNING BOARD

Our question _____

We will change _____

We will measure _____

We will keep _____

these things _____

the same to _____

make our test _____

fair _____

This is the table we will use. (Put in the headings. Fill in the left-hand column.)

We will use _____

these things _____

Task 14

Investigation

How does the amount of detergent affect plant growth?

Ask your teacher about the best types of plant to use in this investigation. Use the same plant for the whole investigation.

✦ Plan your investigation. Use a planning board to help you.

✦ You need to use the following amounts of detergent for your investigation:

Beaker A : 1 teaspoon of detergent
Beaker B : 2 teaspoons of detergent
Beaker C : 3 teaspoons of detergent
Beaker D : 4 teaspoons of detergent
Beaker E : No detergent

✦ Label each beaker.

✦ Stir the solutions well before starting the investigation.

✦ How will you make it a fair test? How will you know how well the plants have grown? Will you:

- count the number of leaves
- measure the height of the plants
- judge how healthy they look?

PCM 11,12

✦ Put your results in a table and draw a graph. Use Photocopy Masters 11 and 12.

✦ What do your results tell you about how detergents affect plant growth?

Fact File

Making ducks waterproof

A duckling would drown if it went straight into the water after it was born. The mother duck makes the duckling's feathers **waterproof** with oil from a **gland** from the bottom of her back. This is called **preening**. Preening makes the feathers waterproof.

Oil spill

Large sea tankers are used to carry oil.

Occasionally, they get damaged and the oil spills into the sea. This can have a terrible effect on the birds who live there. The thick oil clings to their feathers upsetting their natural oils. It needs to be cleaned off or they may die. Detergents are used to clean the oil.

Cleaning feathers

How is oil cleaned from sea or freshwater birds' feathers?
Once their feathers have been cleaned, are the feathers still as useful to the birds?
This test should help you to answer these questions.

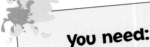

you need:
- some feathers
- cooking oil
- detergent
  e.g. washing-up liquid
- eye-drop pipette

- Dip a feather in cooking oil or use the pipette to put a drop of oil on a feather.

- Gently, rub the oil over the feather.

- Compare a feather with oil and one with no oil. Pour water over them both. Are they both waterproof?

- Wash the feather with oil on it with detergent.

- Let it dry.

- Test to see if it is still waterproof. How do you know?

- What would happen to ducks if they went straight back to the pond after they had been cleaned?

- How should ducks be cared for after they have been cleaned with detergent?

In a pond, some of the animals like pond skaters and whirligig beetles use the surface skin as a place to live and move. What would happen to them if a farmer put detergent on a pond to clean up the oil?

Other effects of detergents on the pond

you need:

- a bowl or large ice cream tub
- water
- tissue paper or kitchen towel
- needle or paper-clip (or talc, see below)
- a used matchstick or cocktail stick
- detergent

① Put the needle or paper-clip on the tissue paper.

② Carefully lower the tissue paper on to the water surface. Let the tissue paper sink to the bottom. Watch. Does the needle float? You may need to try this a few times.

③ Now put a drop of detergent on the end of a used matchstick or cocktail stick.

④ When the needle is floating on the water, touch the surface very carefully with the matchstick. Do this at the edge of the water, away from the needle.

⑤ Watch what happens.

The needle sinks because the detergent destroys the 'skin' in the water's surface.

Normal water surface behaves like a skin. This skin can support things like a needle or small paper-clips.

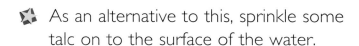

✼ As an alternative to this, sprinkle some talc on to the surface of the water.

✼ Drop in some detergent.

✼ Watch what happens to the talc.